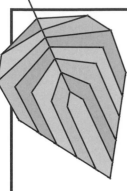

CONNECTRIX

Create stunning geometric works of art by using the arrows to connect a matrix of dots. There are 30 striking pictures to complete, from amazing animals to delicate patterns.

You can complete the puzzles in any colours you like, and why not colour them in once you're done? All the finished pieces are shown at the back of the book.

Here's how to do a Connectrix puzzle:

1. In each puzzle, you can start at whatever dot you like. Each dot has a set of coloured arrows attached to it, which point in different directions.

2. Using a ruler (or anything with a straight edge), follow the line in which the arrow is pointing. You will reach a dot which has an arrow the same colour pointing along the same line. Connect those two dots together with a straight line, from arrow to arrow. You can complete the lines in any colour you want – you might want to do them in pencil or all in black pen. You don't have to match the colour of the arrows.

3. Continue connecting the dots in this way, until there are no more arrows left to match up. Remember to only connect arrows which match in colour and that only point to each other.

Buster Books

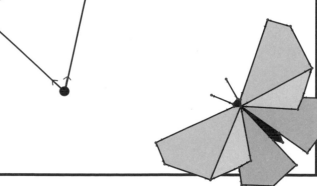

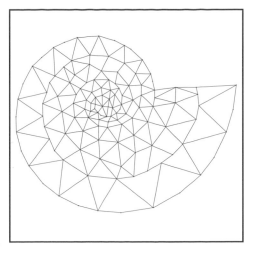
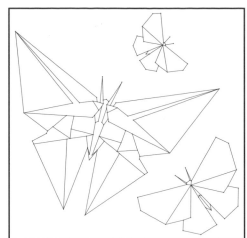
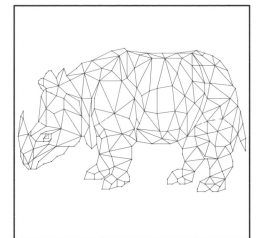

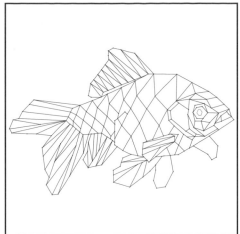

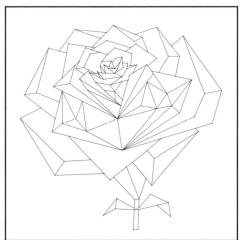

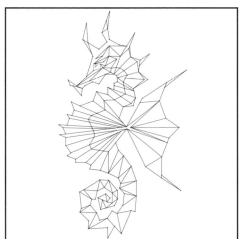

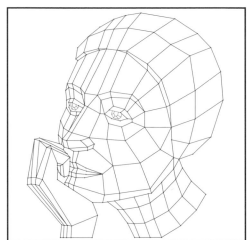

First published in Great Britain in 2017 by Buster Books, an imprint of
Michael O'Mara Books Limited, 9 Lion Yard, Tremadoc Road, London SW4 7NQ

 www.busterbooks.co.uk Buster Children's Books @BusterBooks

Copyright © Buster Books 2017
With material adapted from www.shutterstock.com

A CIP catalogue record for this book is available from the British Library.

ISBN: 978-1-78055-517-1

1 3 5 7 9 10 8 6 4 2

This book was printed in June 2017 by Shenzhen Wing King Tong Paper Products Co. Ltd.,
Shenzhen, Guangdong, China

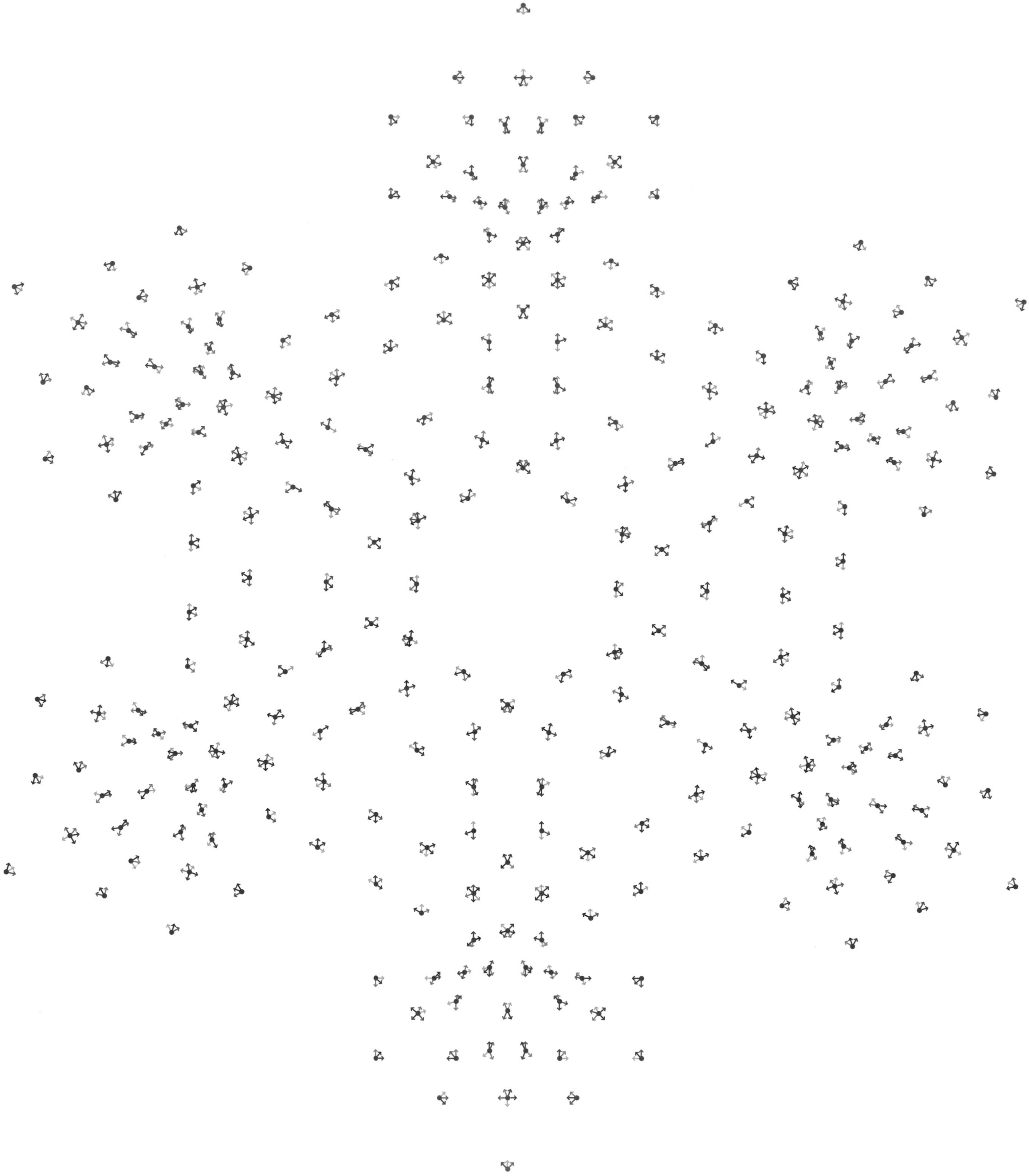

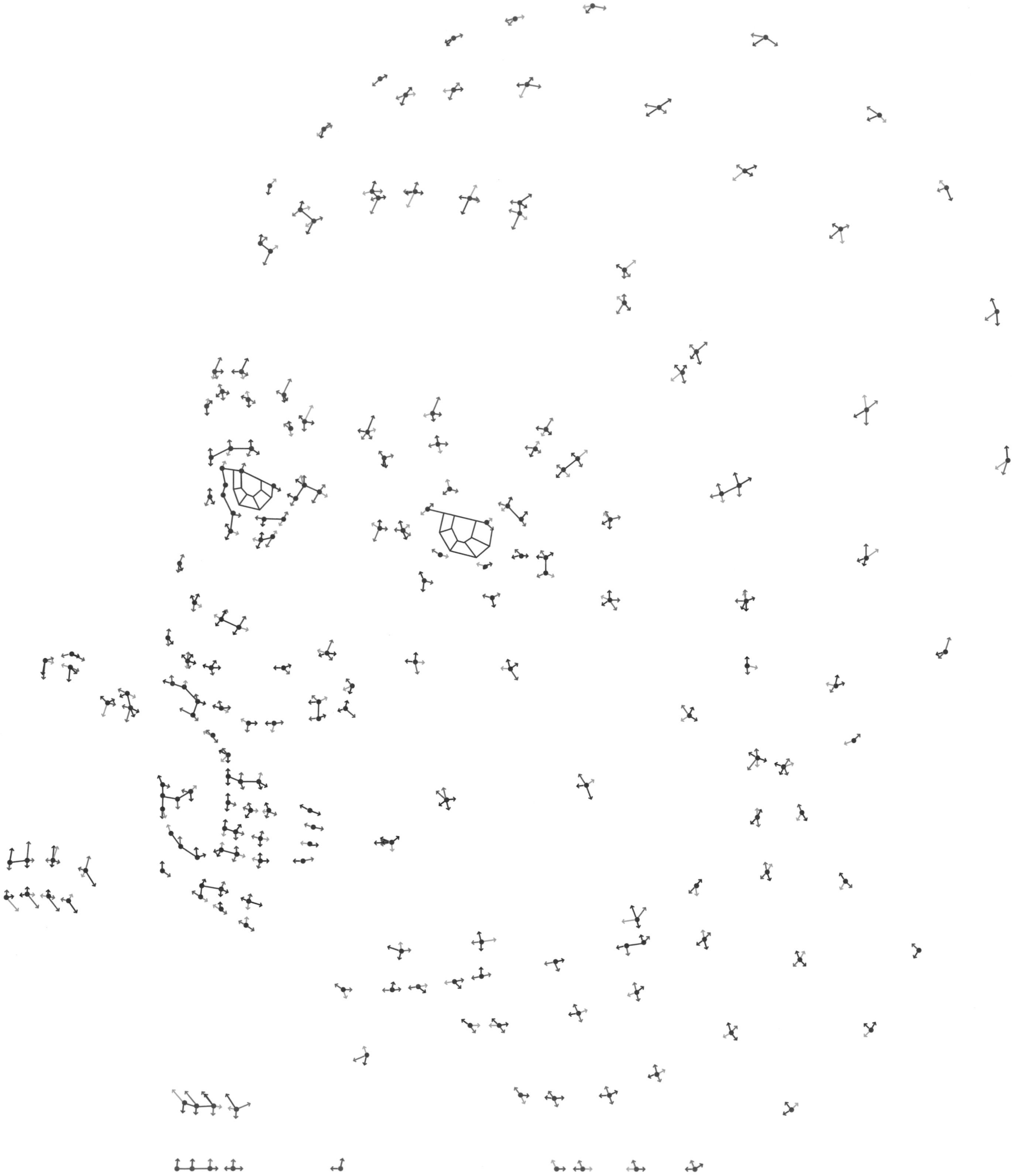

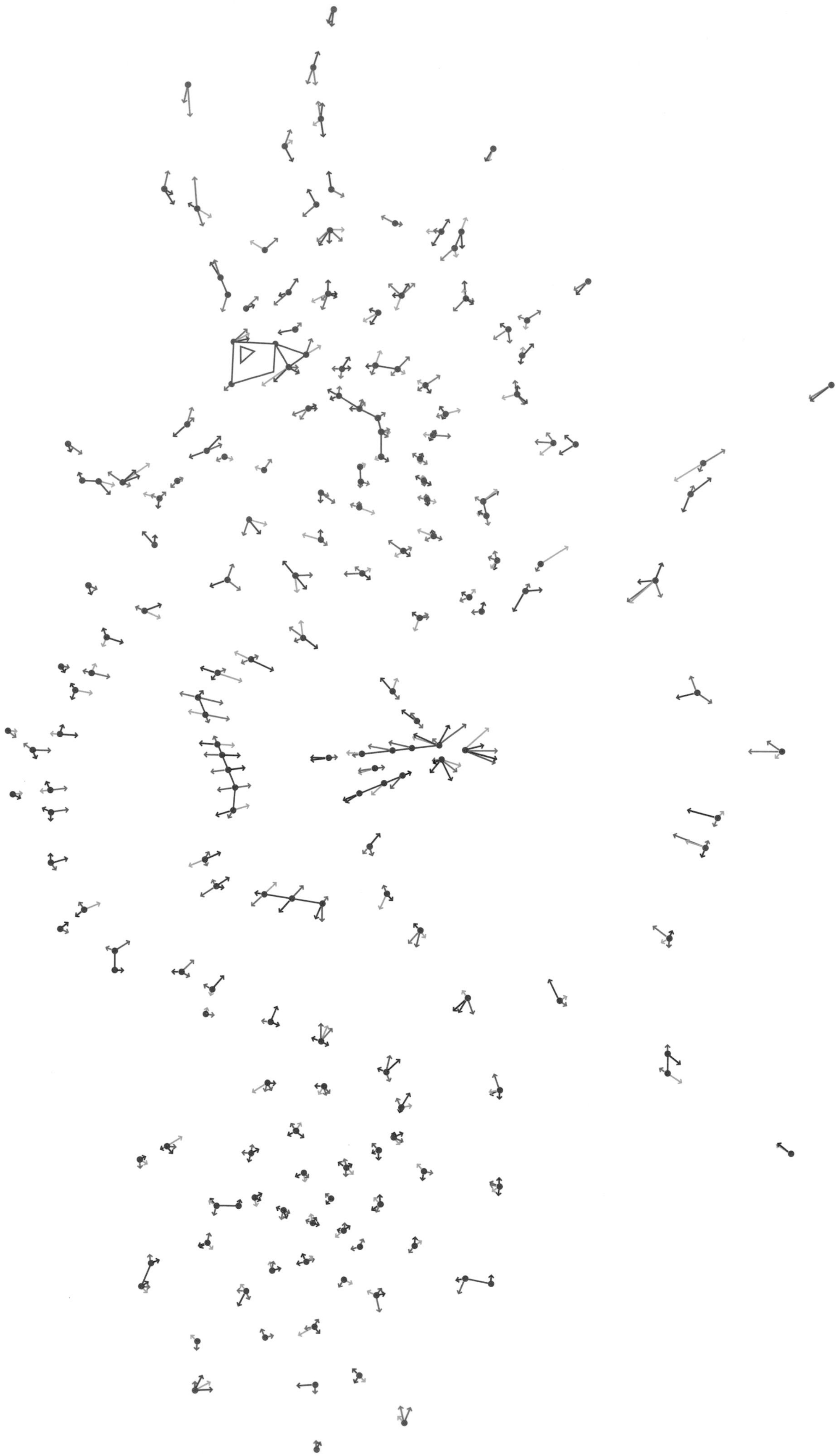

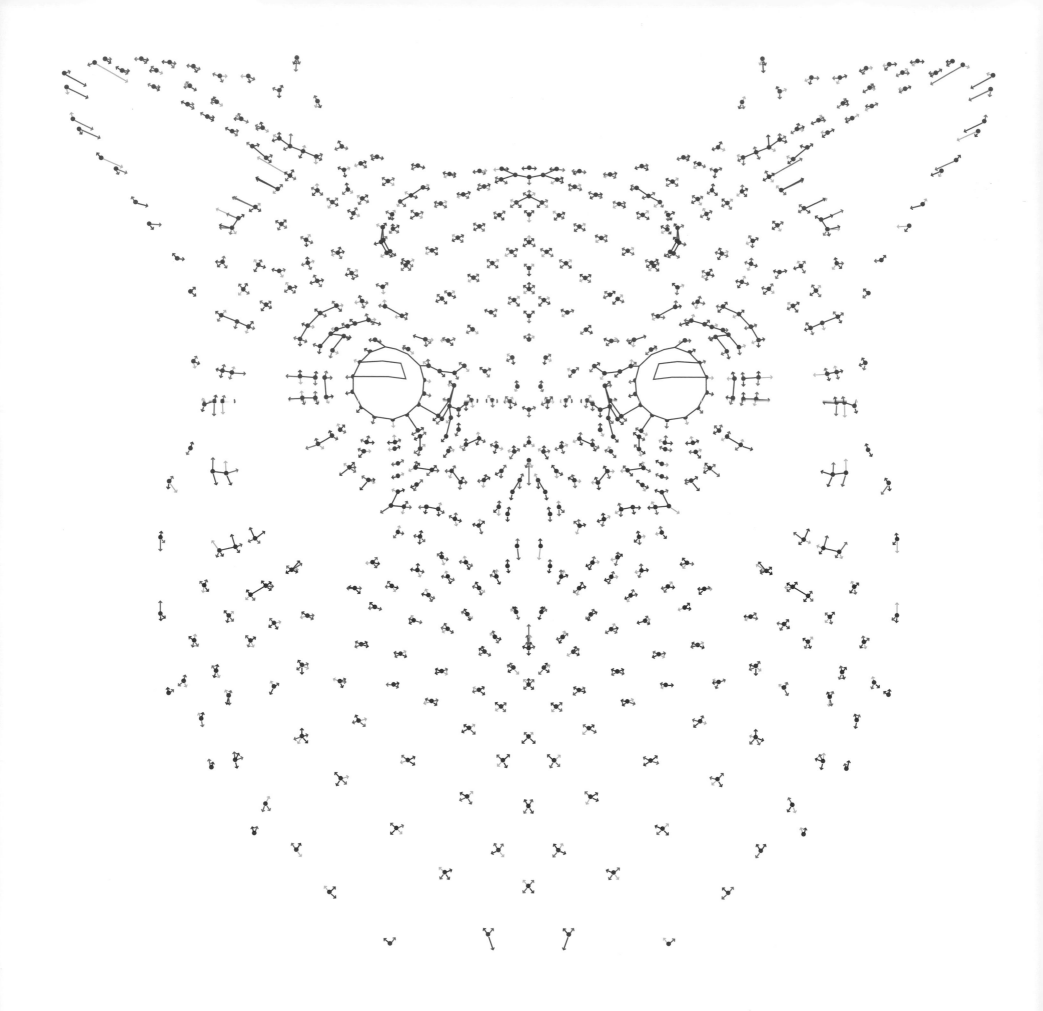

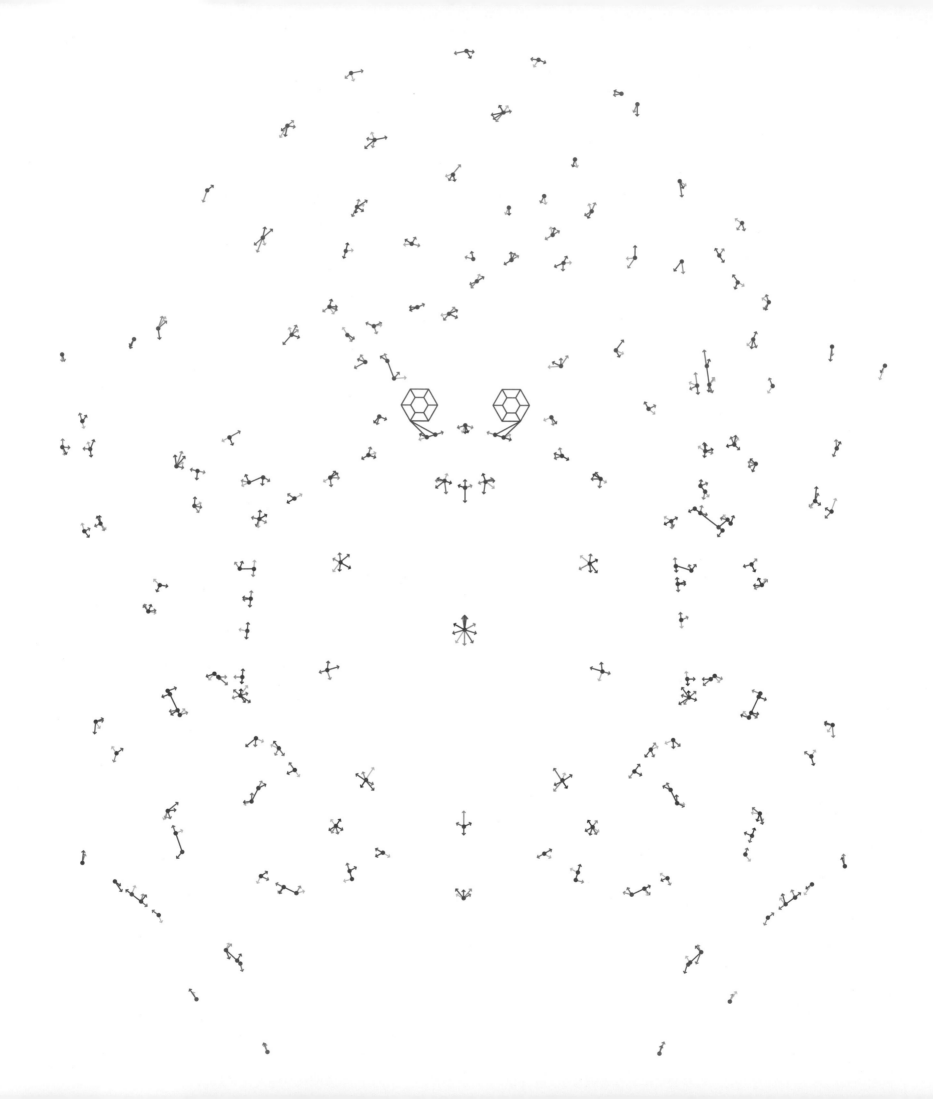

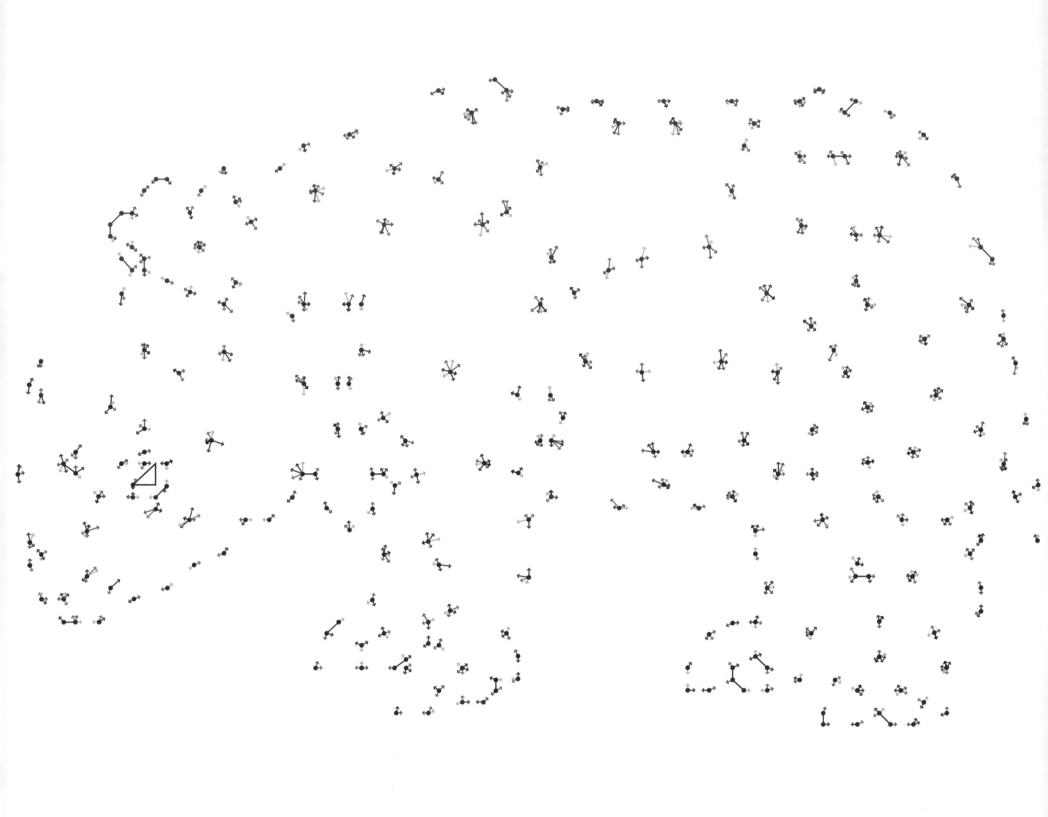

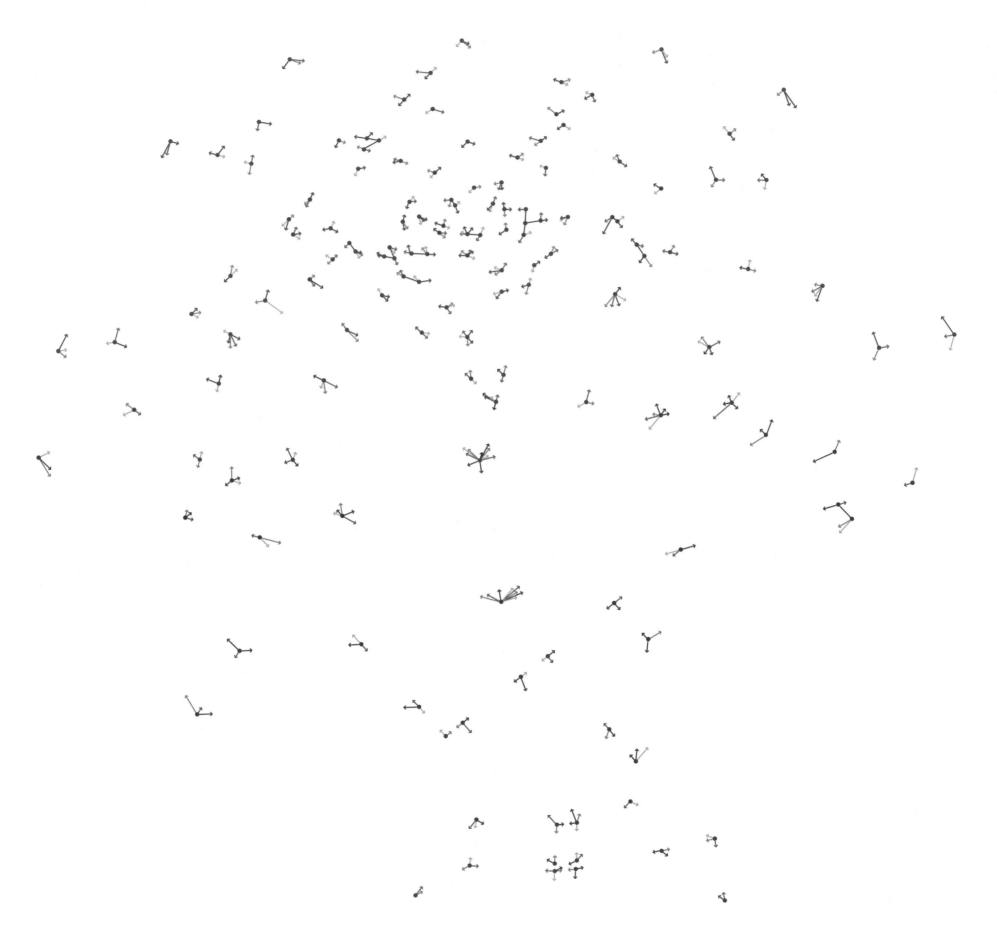

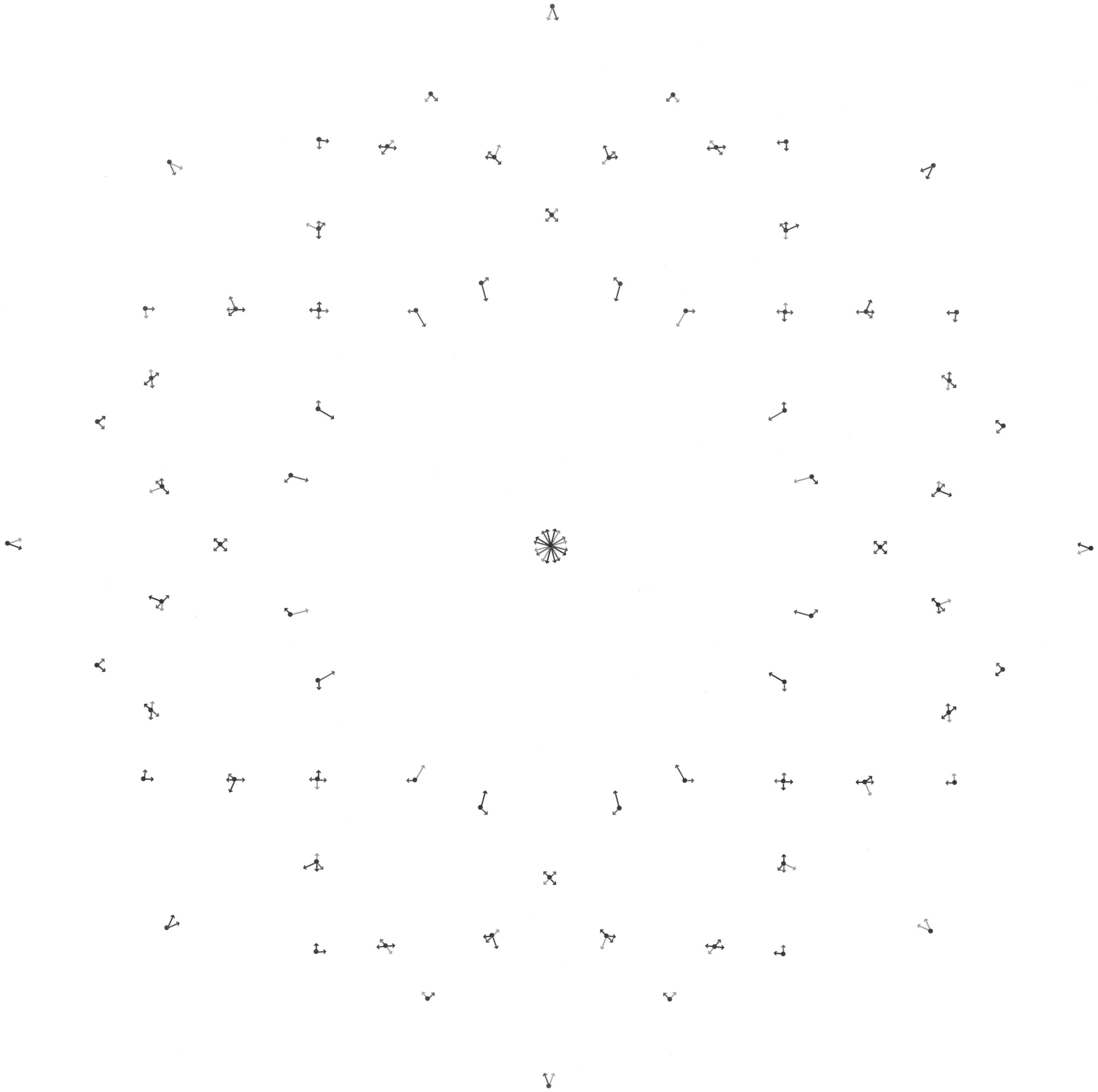

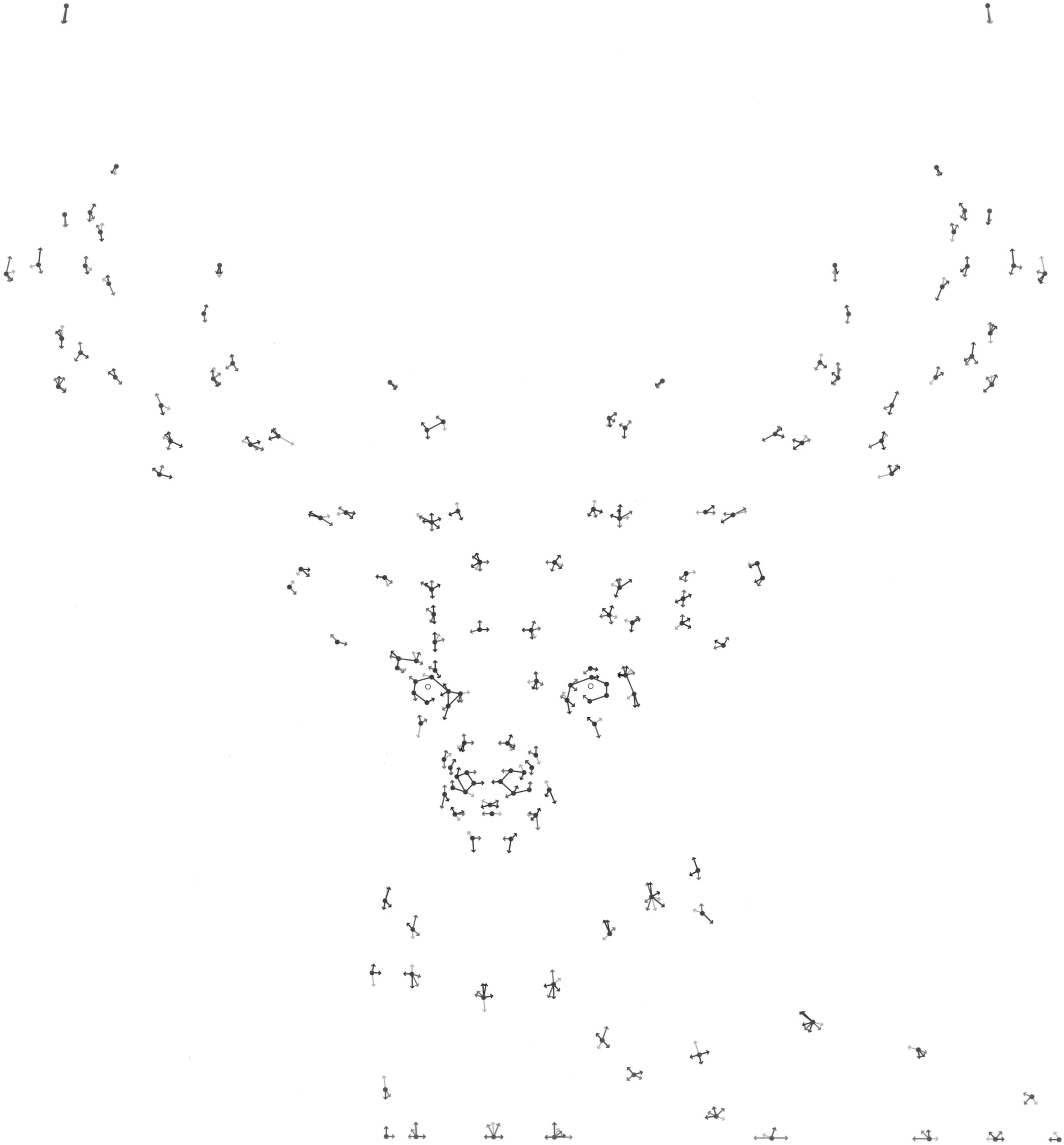

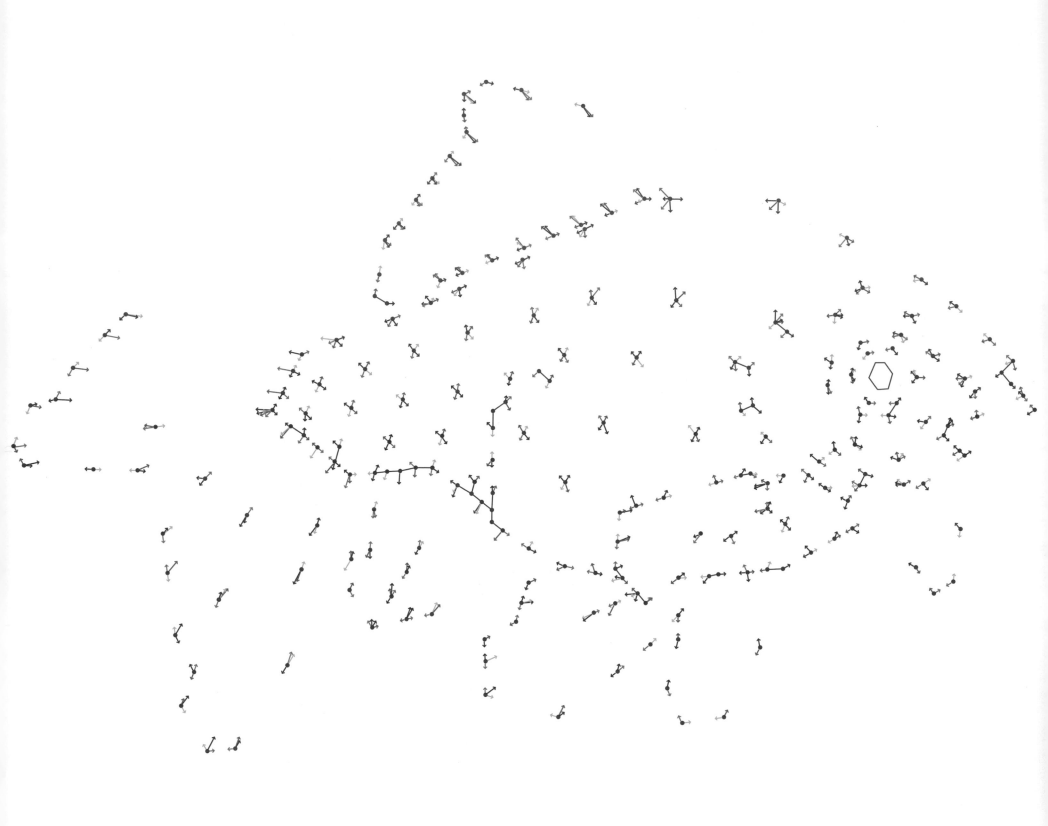

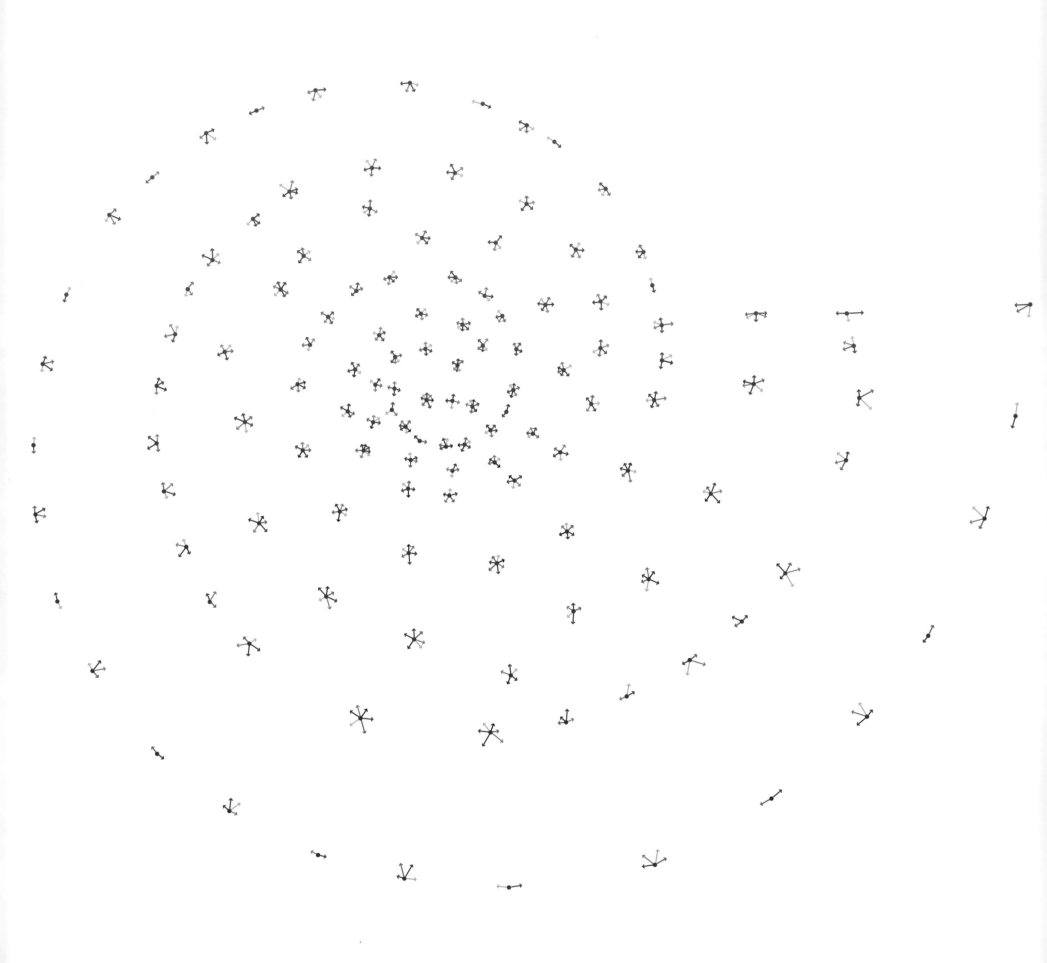

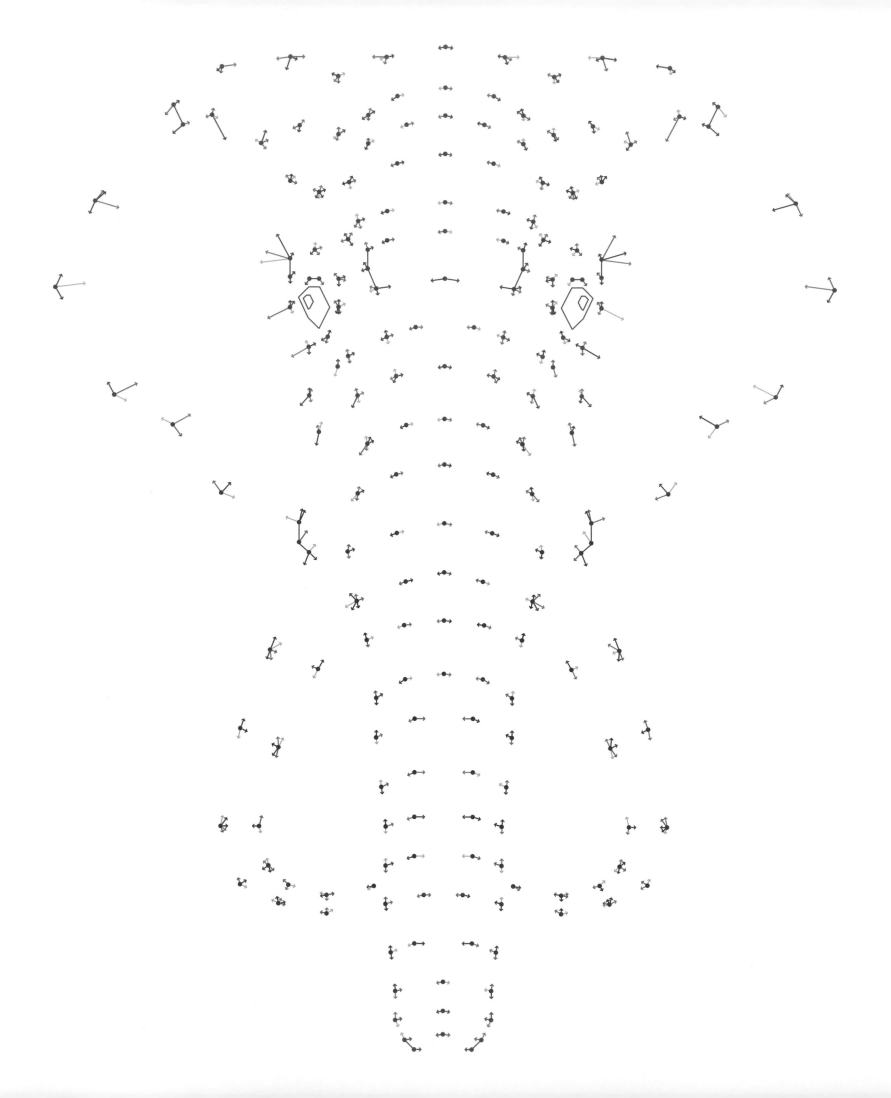

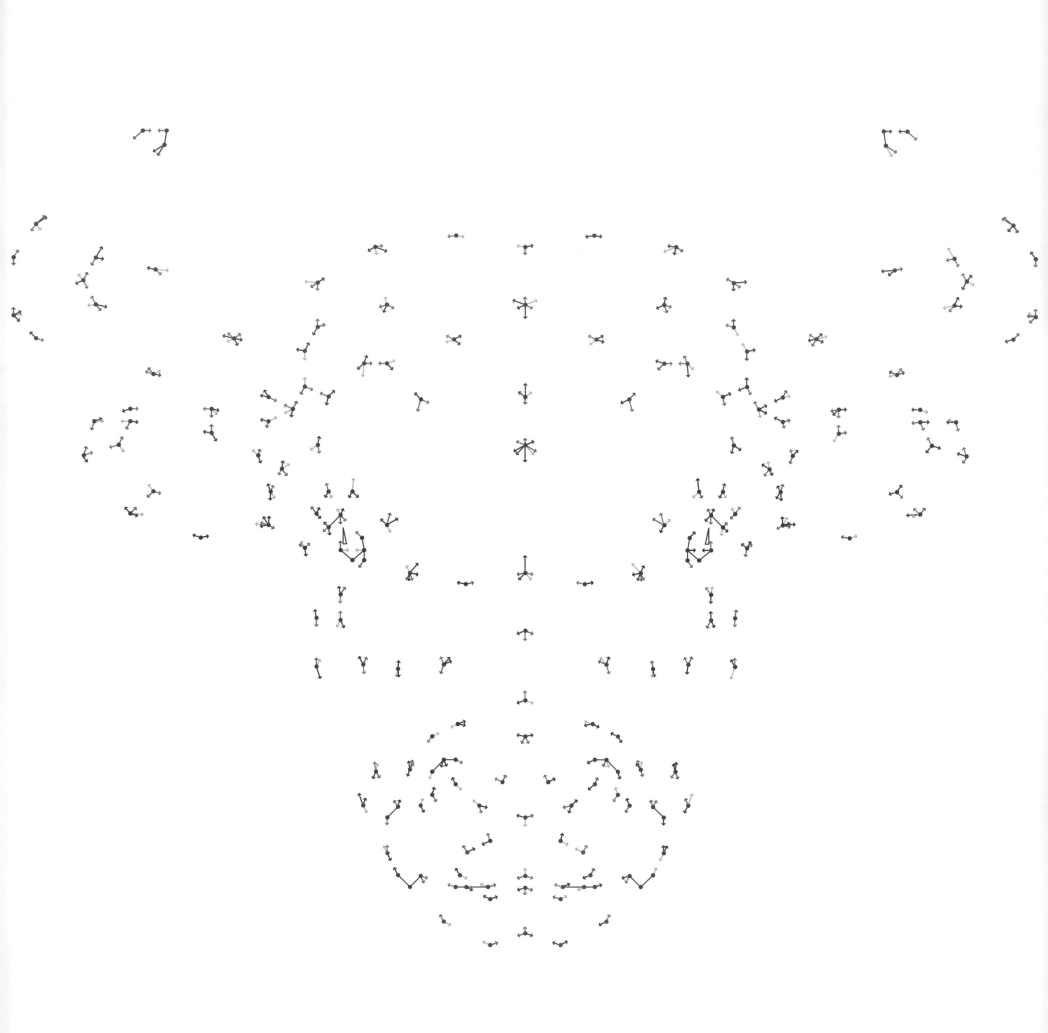

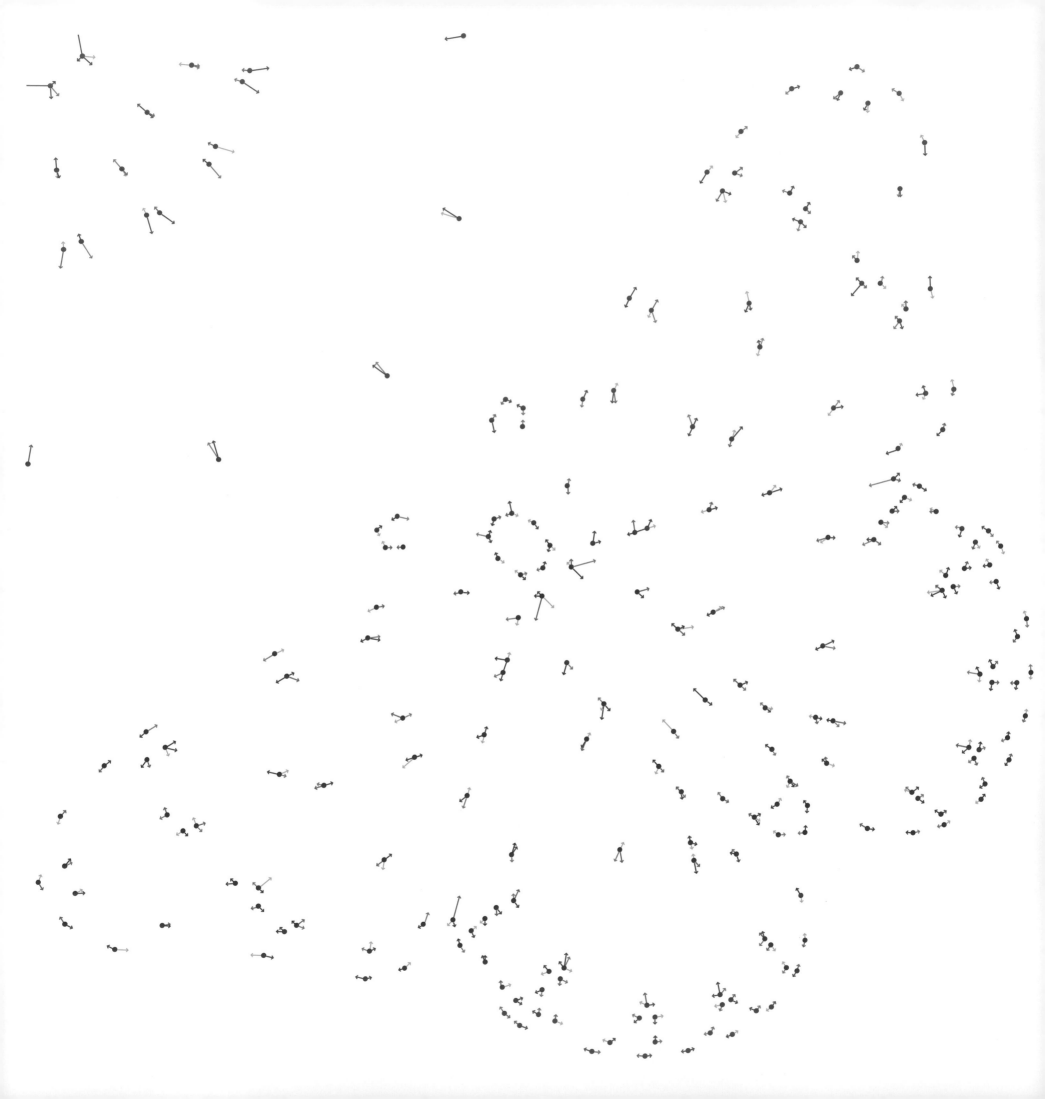

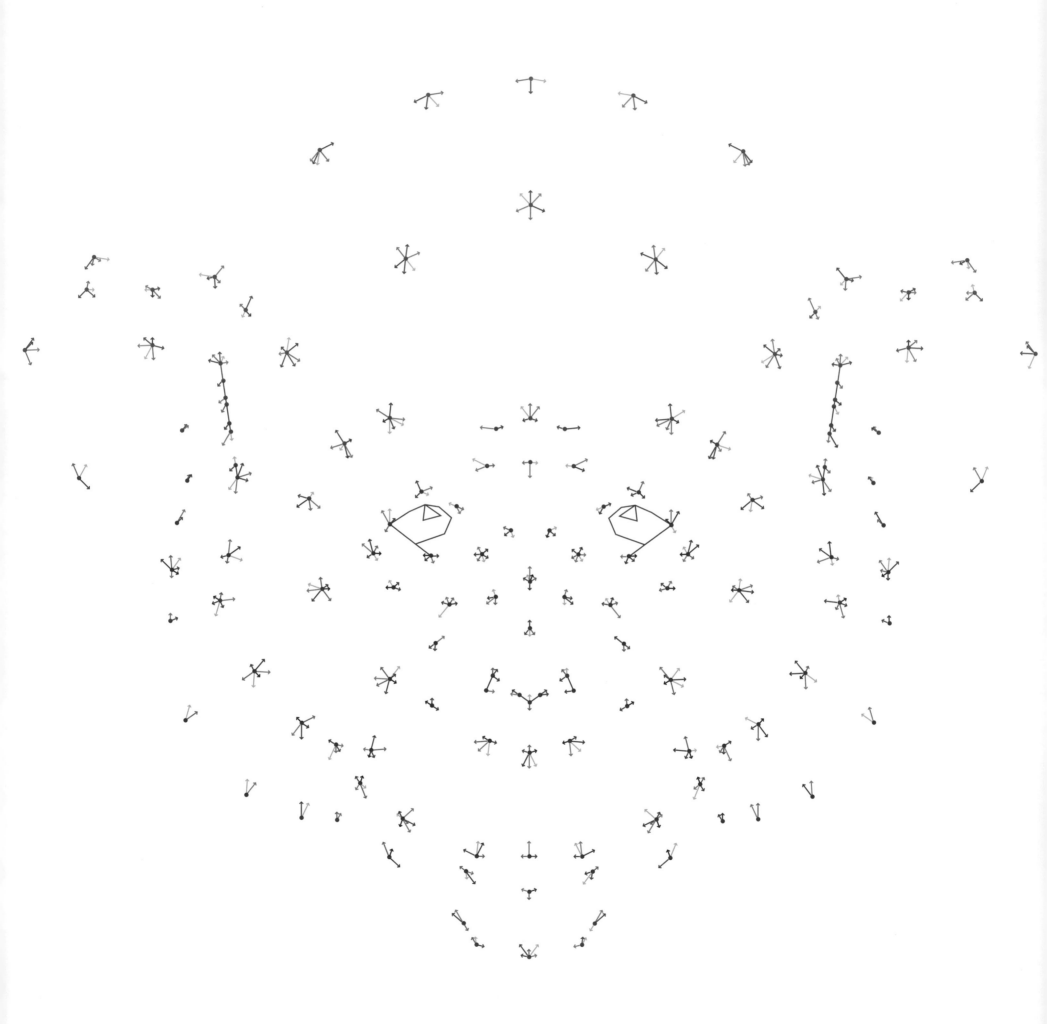

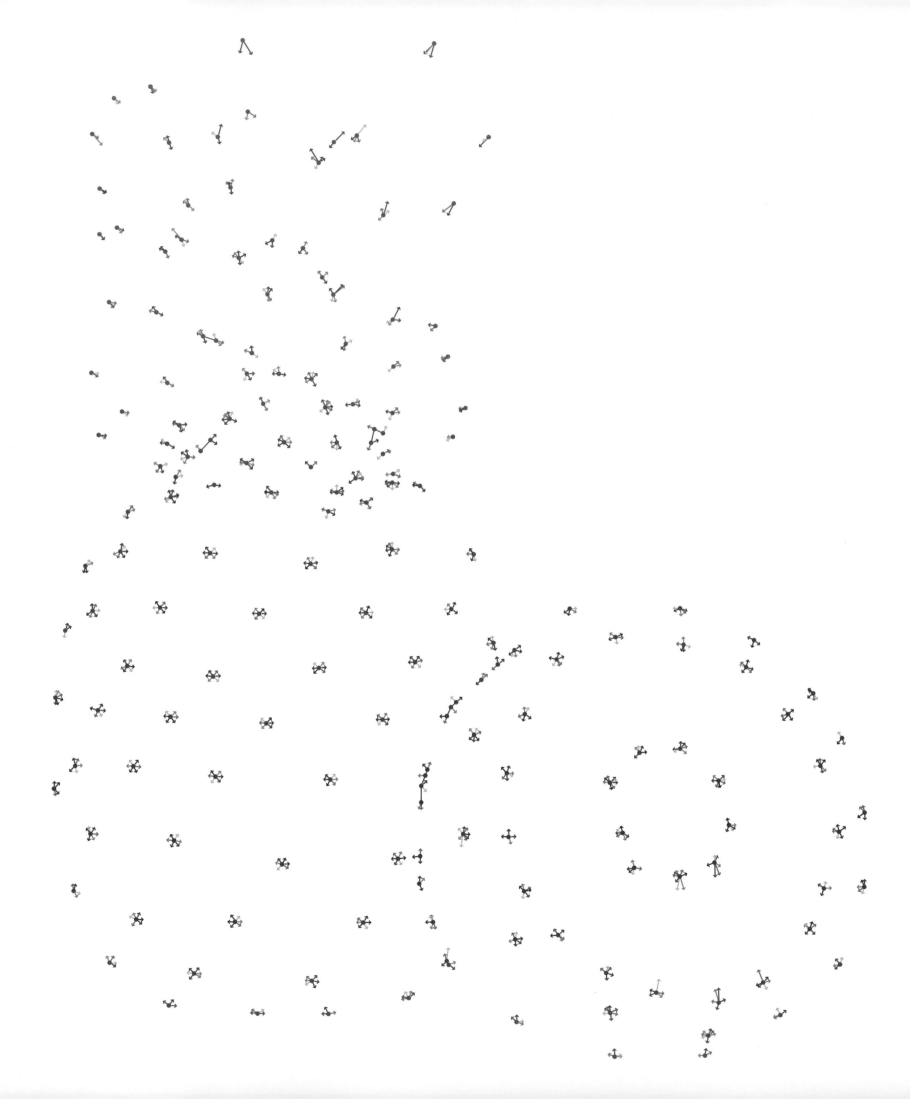

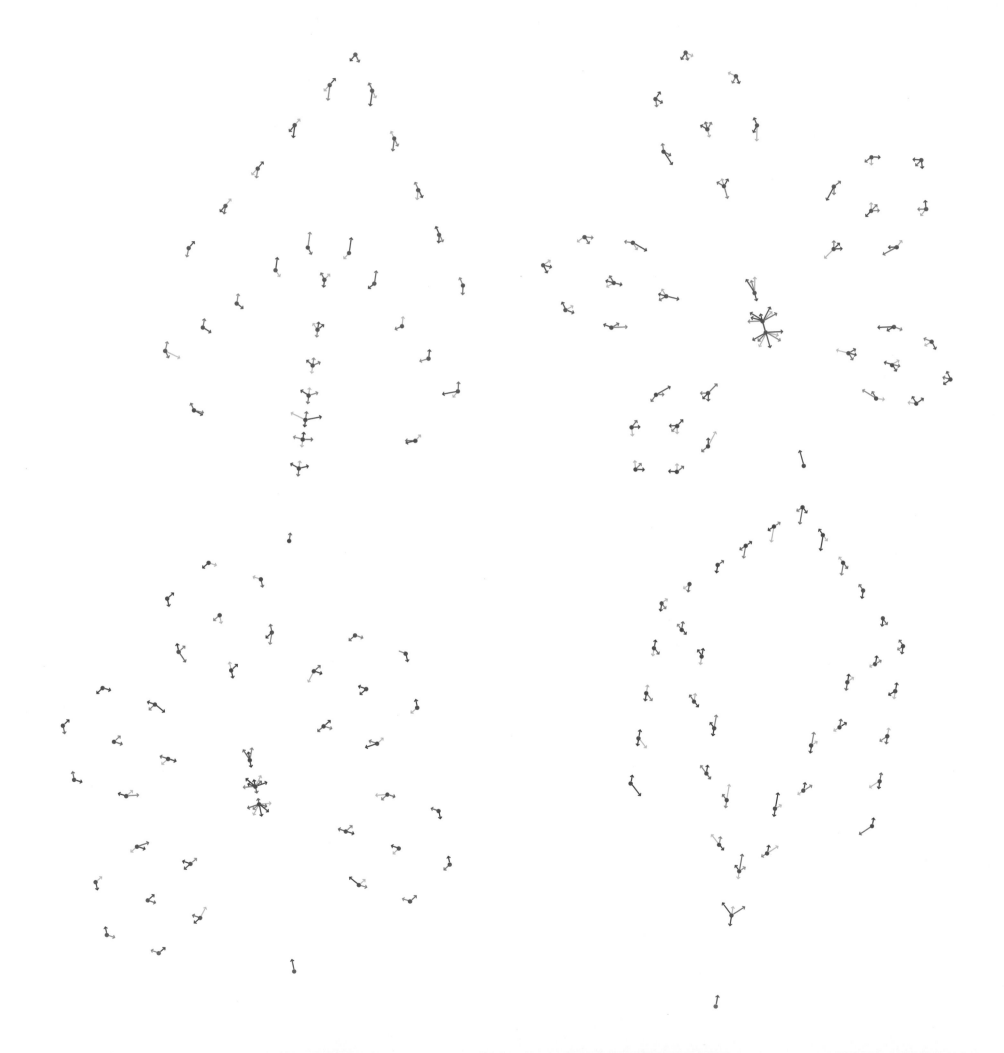

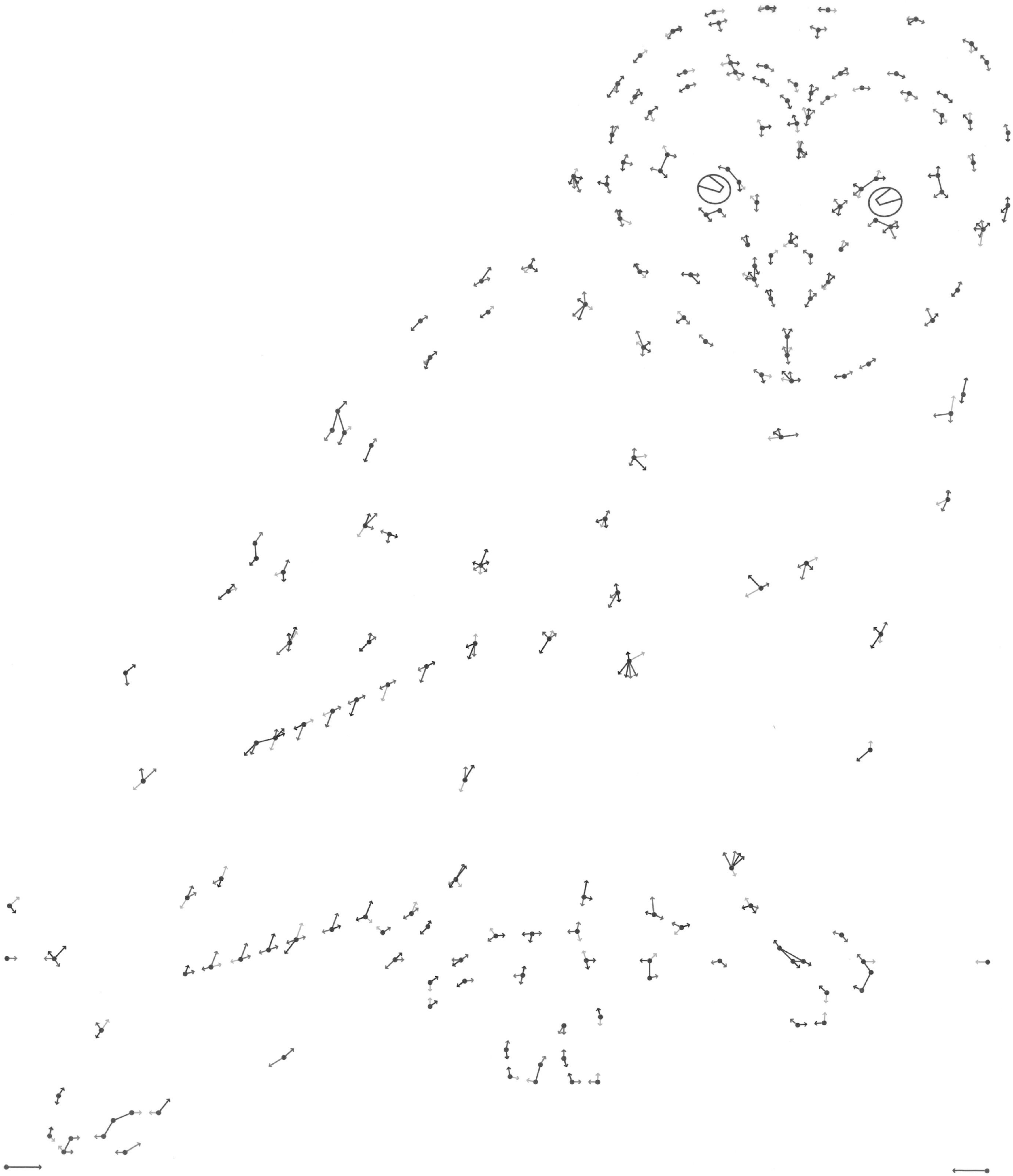

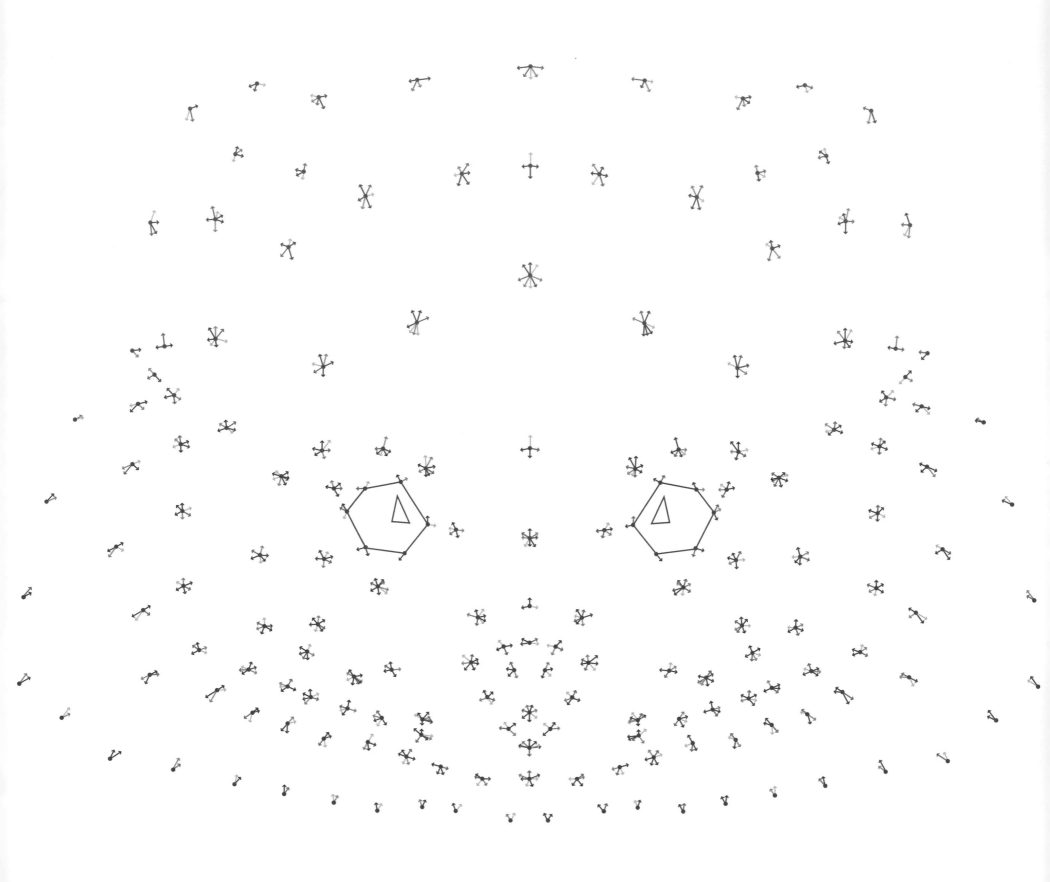

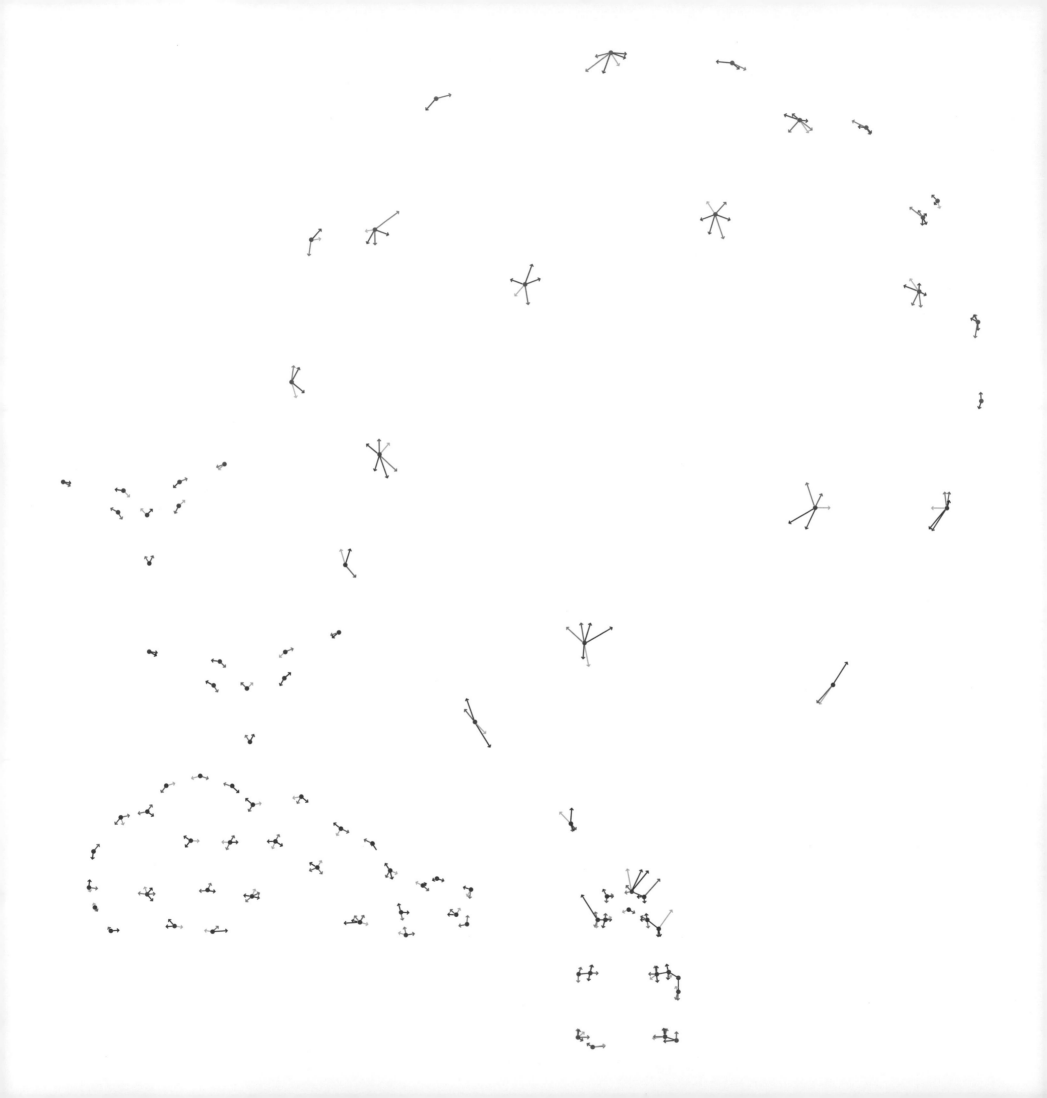

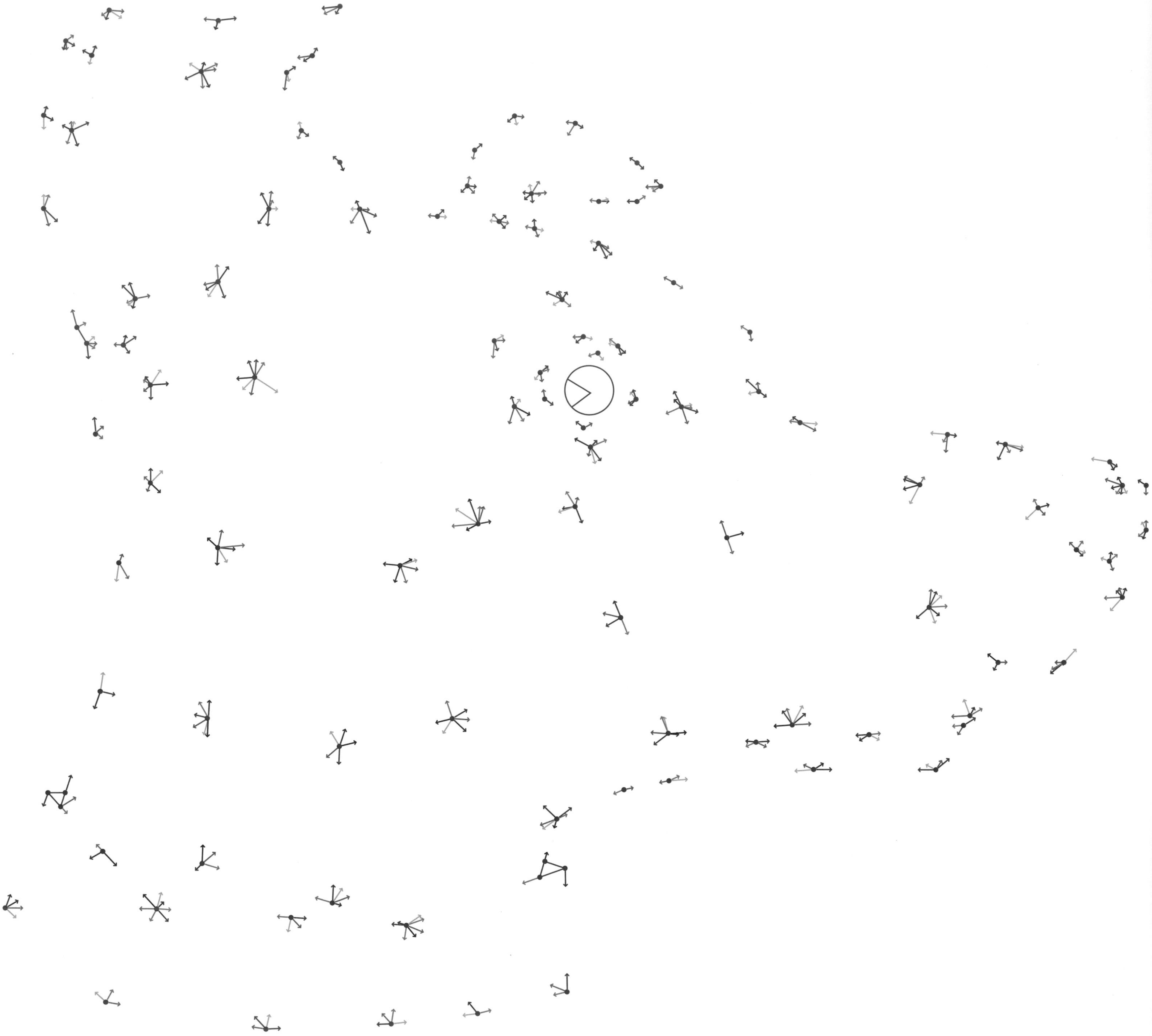

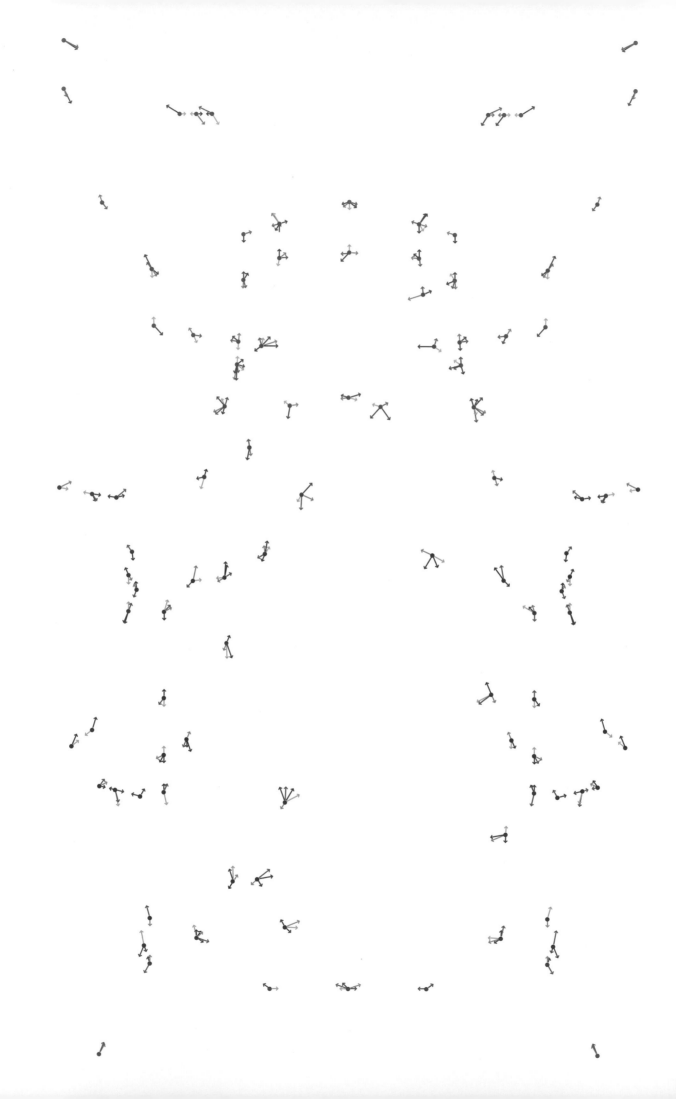